Questioning: An informative skill to have to as an entrepreneur

The Incredible K.S

Copyright

Table of Contents

Crucial questions to ask and their significance

It is impossible to overstate the importance of asking questions in both your professional and personal life. Questions have an impact on almost every aspect of our lives and careers. To discuss why it is important to ask why, I have gathered research, statistics, ideas, and thoughts from people and brands all over the world. The project 100 Good Questions, which focuses on posing 100 questions to help with your life, career, and other issues, was just launched.

One of the smartest things you can do, ironically, is to be willing to ask 'dumb' questions. According to Allen Gannett, author of The Creative Curve, "learning the fundamentals of a field or craft is frequently where people get stuck, but being willing to ask the fundamental questions helps you build a foundation for the advanced parts of a skill.

"Asking someone to share their experiences, insights, or passions with you leads to a connection and frequently to fondness, which is a strong foundation for enduring relationships. The way that people have come to feel close to me based solely on the questions I've posed has been both surprising and lovely. According to television and comic book writer Amanda Deibert, it has resulted in genuine friendships and even jobs.

Powerful inquiries typically have the potential to transform or expand a career or business from the inside out.

"Simple inquiries can have a big impact. Thinking is sparked by the question "Why?" Innovation is fueled by asking "Why not?" "explains Nathan Young, 600 & Rising's co-founder and marketing consultant.

The habit of asking "why?" has served me the best throughout my entire career, according to producer and author Katie Martell.

Remember when you were younger and asking questions and being curious were just part of interacting with the world? The adults in our lives were frequently perplexed by our constant "why" and "how" questions. Children gradually learn as they mature that providing answers is more significant, whether it be in the form of exams, interviews, or the capacity to participate in a conversation. As we get older, we stop challenging the people and environment around us. It turns out, according to the Harvard Business Review, that many adults with kids believe that between 70 and 80 percent of their kids' conversations consisted of questions. The estimate for adults was between 15 and 25 percent.

"Children frequently ask "why" to comprehend context. Which raises the question of why adults don't use that same sense of critical inquiry in their careers. Any strategic framework should start by identifying the "why." Why are you solving this problem? You will never be successful at what if you don't repeatedly ask yourself why "suggests SalientMG CEO Erin (Mack) McKelvey.

"Recently, my oldest daughter admitted she dislikes asking questions in class because she fears people won't think she's intelligent. I informed her that, more often than not, it's those who pose the questions who are the smartest in the room. In my line of work, we can help businesses overcome plateaus by asking the right questions carefully. To find what you can test to unlock new growth, William Harris, CEO of eCommerce growth agency Elumynt, suggests asking questions until there are no more answers.

Given the sharp decline in adult question-asking, it is understandable why so many people are searching for tips on how to ask better questions, more frequently. According to research, asking more questions increases emotional intelligence, which improves soft skills that are essential for leadership at work and developing interpersonal relationships.

A good way to improve ourselves is to ask questions.

"My sense of curiosity has assisted me in making sense of the world. Anna Melissa, a free-lance content strategist, says, "I believe that once we stop asking ourselves important questions, we stifle our progress and put a cap on our understanding.

"I find it helpful to periodically ask myself internal questions. Am I producing content that piques my interest? What current projects give me the most elation, and how can I start taking on more of those kinds of tasks? Am I effectively using my time, or should I look into outsourcing? Do I require more slumber? (Yes!) According to Robin Eisenberg, an artist at @robineisenberg, "I think it's good to check in with yourself every so often to get a sense of how you're feeling creatively, professionally, and personally."

Group morale rises when more questions are asked because doing so deepens understanding and enables teams to collaborate more effectively to find better solutions. People who ask questions are more adept at developing relationships, which can be applied to branding strategy to increase success in creating a strong personal brand.

When I reflect on my career and life to date, I see that the depth of my accomplishments and victories have been closely related to the importance I placed on the kinds of questions I was willing to ponder. I was able to go further with bettTos, says entrepreneur Olori Swank.

"I've realized that I always get what I ask for in life. As a journalist, when I interview famous people and industry leaders, I make it a point to pose challenging questions. To speak up for me and obtain the opportunities I deserve, I pose even more probing questions behind the scenes. Since I now run my own media business, I lead by using the persuasive power of questions. I'm giving my team the chance to practice their problem-solving abilities by posing questions. Over time, they develop a great deal of independence and resourcefulness in overcoming challenges, according to XiXi Yang, host of "Pop News Edition" and CEO of XYZ Media.

Building relationships starts with questions

In his renowned self-help book, How to Win Friends and Influence People, Dale Carnegie advised readers nearly a century ago, "Ask questions the other person will enjoy answering." For many years, research from all over the world has suggested that the goal of asking questions in conversation is to exchange information or manage impressions.

Timelapse photographer Matthew Vandeputte says, "Using polls and asking questions of my audience helps me to understand them better, which ultimately brings us closer and creates a deeper and more meaningful relationship."

"I've built my entire career around posing queries to artists. Before conducting an interview, as a journalist and on-camera host, I do extensive research and brainstorm new questions, making surc that a) thc qucstion hasn't been asked before and b) the coercive to telling their overall story. In addition, Shirley Ju, a journalist and on-camera host at @shirju, says that questions are crucial to getting through and discovering the underlying traumas that feed into your present-day struggles.

"There is no progress without learning. I make it a point to constantly quench my thirst for knowledge because I believe it is foolish for any of us to believe we are experts in everything. "I make it a point to feed that fire, ensuring that I never stop on the quest to know, experience, and understand more," says Karen Civil, media maven and co-host of Girl I Guess Podcast. "Where there is a flicker of curiosity there is the beginning of a flame fueled by information.

Asking questions works both in work and in life.

In other words, asking questions serves to help people learn from each other, and become more likable. In one study, researchers asked one pool of participants to ask at least nine questions in fifteen minutes, and the other pool of participants to ask no more than four questions in fifteen minutes. Participants were randomly paired up in the form of speed dating and online chats.

The outcomes? Online chat partners liked the participants more when they asked more questions, and speed daters were more likely to request a second date. Participants felt more respected and heard when more questions were asked, which increased their sense of intimacy and understanding. According to a different study, curious people generally make better friends. "People disclose more, share more, and return the favor by asking questions of you when you show curiosity and you inquire about them and learn something interesting about them," claims Todd Kashdan, a researcher of the psychology of curiosity.

According to Mike Allton, Brand Evangelist at Agorapulse, "Asking open questions of peers and colleagues, and giving them the space to answer, has helped me to build rapport with them which, over the years, has led to countless relationships and opportunities."

"It's important to ask the right questions. It was essential for me to inquire when I was creating my line of fragrances. There are a lot of crucial moving parts that can make or break your product or service. When adding new responsibilities to your business, there will always be a learning curve, but asking questions up front and before committing significant sums of money will help avoid many headaches later, according to Alexia P. Ammonds, founder of Eat.Sweat.Undress.

Questions are effective because they can lead to transformation. Giving information and facts is useful, but asking questions can change one's perspective, spur creativity, and produce real change within an organization, according to Stephanie Liu, founder of Captivate on Command.

How does any of this relate to the development and use of personal brands? Consider some of the branding tenets from the past. Genuine brands want to tell their story in their own words and for others to do the same. People ask each other more questions to appear genuine and likeable. The same is true for good brands; interact and engage your audience.

Because there are so many moving parts in real estate investing, it is crucial to ask questions. Something that seems straightforward can completely alter a transaction, turning a profit into a loss. A lot of hassles and potential loss can be avoided by being aware of the specifics of a transaction. The founder of Nuurez, Inc., Noelle Randall, says, "I try to arm my students with different scenarios and tactics as a coach so that they can see the unexpected before it causes issues.

"If I hadn't hired people with intellectual curiosity, I most definitely wouldn't have been able to create Epidemic Sound. To ensure that we're always moving forward with the best possible solution for our customers, company, and people, I make it my mission to create an internal environment where people can question the status quo and direction of the business. According to Oscar Hoglund, co founder and CEO of Epidemic Sound, "It's such a simple technique but it can go a long way in helping you build a company or achieve success in a certain area.

By encouraging the community that supports your brand to continue sharing your brand story, asking questions can help you build that community. Your brand can develop once it starts asking questions and paying attention.

The Development of Emotional Intelligence Through Questioning

A curious mind is a mind that has emotional intelligence. Some people naturally possess the capacity for good questioning, which is rooted in a curious mindset. If asking questions isn't something you do naturally, don't let that deter you.

"Saying what I want has always been one of my biggest fears. The fear of "being difficult" has brought on the anxiety that goes along with it. According to Krystina Arielle, host of Star Wars: The High Republic Show on starwars.com,

"When I started my career in entertainment, I decided I would ask questions, not to be difficult, but because I deserve to have all the information that enables me to do the best possible job that I can do.

The more questions you ask, the better you get at asking them, according to research. And the more inquiries we make, the more adept we become at developing our social abilities. Increased emotional intelligence can result in a variety of advantages, many of which take the form of soft skills that enable us to advance from being followers to leaders at work and in our communities.

"I regularly interact with interns and externs, and we firmly advise them to ask questions during their orientations, workshops, and job interviews. All parties involved gain from asking questions, which can also act as a guide for many important conversations. Whether or not we agree with the answer to a question, we must use the insightful information to guide our decision-making. Trina Terrell-Andrews, CEO of the Mark Cuban Heroes Basketball Center, says that when we don't question something, we run the risk of assuming or jumping to conclusions.

"Questions are the Google of the world," someone once said. Asking questions will help you find the solution to an unknown, according to Quiana McDaniel, founder of The House of Dasha and Dasha Cosmetics.

We get better at asking the right questions as we ask more questions. Harvard Business Review breaks this down into four types of questions: Clarifying, Adjoining, Funneling, and Elevating. Each question type helps the conversationalist achieve a different goal: clarifying questions helps to understand others better.

“Learning to ask the following questions has helped me so much in both personal and professional life... how long do I have to do this? What do you need me to do/what format do you want this in? Why are we doing (project/show) this? or Why are you asking me specifically to do/say THING? It lets me know why someone wants me to do a thing and most importantly how they expect me to deliver on the aid thing. I've wasted a lot of time on things I shouldn't have been doing before I understood how critical it was to ask questions. Tanya DePass, creator and creative director of Into the Mother Lands

RPG and @cypheroftyr, says, "I always ask these first.

We can view issues or subjects from a different perspective by using accompanying questions. Intimate and non-intimate topics are explored in greater depth by spiraling questions. Elevating questions advances the discussion and enables us to see the bigger picture. Asking the right questions improves as our emotional intelligence increases.

Never be reluctant to seek information. Admitting you don't have all the answers is not a sign of weakness because nobody does. The opposite of being smart is missing out on the chance to learn from others due to fear, laziness, or the conviction that you know it all. The smart person is self-assured enough to ask questions and seek answers. You don't, Lia Haberman, the adjunct instructor at UCLAx, reveals in advance.

We develop our emotional intelligence by asking questions.

Strong emotional intelligence assists us in building a positive relationship with our audience and communities when it comes to our brand. Asking questions not only engages the audience and enables us to hear what they have to say, but it also enables us to determine how to develop our brand. By asking questions, brands can better understand their target market, figure out how to serve them, and keep the big picture in mind. We become better brands as a result of developing our emotional intelligence, both in terms of crafting effective messaging and having a positive effect on our communities.

"Research your topic. Asking the right questions can help you learn something useful, intimate, or thought-provoking. That transforms a surfacc-lcvcl convcrsation into onc that is sincere and real. Finding out what makes someone tick and ignites a spark is my favorite part of every interview, says Jessie Maltin, co host and producer of Maltin On Movies.

Sincere curiosity is the starting point for the art of storytelling. I imagine myself as a journalist when I interview clients, asking pertinent and well-timed questions to build a compelling story. The most authentic and compelling videos, podcasts, and communications—across all mediums—are produced when preparation is done in advance of an interview, says Cathy

Landtroop, chief communications officer of Vista Bank.

Posing Questions Encourages a Positive Work Environment

Researchers have figured out why we become less curious as we age, changing from being inquisitive kids to less inquisitive adults. In essence, we as individuals and groups are rewarded for providing answers in school, the workplace, and the home. We were taught in school to respond to questions on tests and quizzes. To improve our employment eligibility, we must first go through a lengthy interview phase. Supervisors anticipate that once we start working, we will find solutions to various work-related problems. We may jump to conclusions rather than consider issues in their full context if we ask fewer questions and are less inquisitive.

"As a small business owner or entrepreneur, it's crucial to inquire about the media or press coverage you are seeking, particularly concerning how your story is being presented. You can feel at ease and make sure that your values and brand messaging are being communicated by asking for interview questions or the angle that the outlet, TV stations, or interviewer is pursuing in advance, according to Leah Frazier, CEO and Publicist, Think Three Media.

"The strength and value of a good question can enable you to humbly demonstrate your craft's expertise. The only way to learn information that will lead to a better understanding, whether it be your day job—which for me is healthcare—or diving into entrepreneurship with your various start-up companies, says Lukwon Mack, founder of M Case.

"When I was a young child working for my immigrant mother's small business, I discovered that I liked to pass the time by asking questions...

I soon discovered that I was naturally curious and enjoyed finding out more about other people and my surroundings. Now, a big part of my job as a journalist is to ask questions. News anchor Frances Wang says, "I like to think that my personality, passion, and purpose are all intertwined.

Particularly when speaking with managers and large groups of people, asking questions can frequently make us feel exposed. Asking questions can make us feel as though we appear to be less informed because we are taught to have the right response. But as we've covered in great detail in this article, asking questions has a lot of advantages. In a work setting, it can lead to better decision making and a corporate culture that welcomes the exchange of ideas. Businesses and organizations should adopt a new work culture where asking questions is the norm because the more questions we ask, the more adept we become at asking the right questions.

"I learned to be okay with asking stupid questions, which was the most valuable lesson I took away. By asking the right questions, I've been able to discover insights that would have taken me years to discover, unlock entrances I never even knew existed, and do so much more. According to Sydney Liu, CEO of Commaful, "Commaful was founded and is where it is today because of the answers to many important questions from community members, writers, readers, investors, friends, and more.

In the bigger picture of brand strategy, asking questions within a company or organization is just as significant as asking them of your target market. It enables staff to enquire into the rationale behind the operation of specific procedures and gain a deeper comprehension of the overall goal of the workplace. Being able to ask questions internally, for example, can keep a brand that promotes sustainability on course. We get better at living our brand when we start to wonder about it and delve into the meaning behind it. And a brand that grows is one that fully embraces its narrative and its core values.

According to Dr. Kimberly Ellison, an international speaker and consultant, "Asking questions is critical to the success and sustainability of your outcomes in the world of professional development and training."

Each significant discovery begins with a question. When customers inquire about our luxury event rentals, they open themselves up to countless options and possibilities for their event that they might not even have thought were possible. According to Laura Fote, owner of L&B Concepts, "When people don't ask questions, it leaves room for assumptions and chaos."

So, is your brand prepared to pique interest?

Co-Founder of SAPPHIRE Thomas Ma says, "If you don't ask, you won't know the outcome to what you are seeking."

Every individual brand has much to learn about developing curiosity. We know that every good brand knows how to foster and build relationships with their audience, and the science shows that asking questions is key for this.

As we ask more questions, we allow others to feel heard and understood, allowing us to be more likable overall. As a brand asks more questions, it becomes more emotionally intelligent and aware of messaging that resonates with the people we are trying to reach. Brands need to be equally inquisitive and attentive internally in addition to being so externally. Is your company's or organization's brand personality present in every department or is it just a front for customers and clients? Brands can start to develop and grow when they become curious about their own procedures and the audience they serve.

Being informal

Even the best of us experience this: we're speaking with a new person, and the conversation is lagging. We're at a loss for how to proceed and where to go, and the awkward silence is getting to us. Even though these moments don't matter much in the big scheme of things, they can still be very stressful for you when they do.

The fact that you might miss the chance to get to know a great person because you don't know how to carry on a conversation effectively is, in my opinion, more problematic than that awkward feeling.

It is typical for conversations with new people to start awkwardly. If you can help them get past those hiccups, you might be able to start a lovely relationship.

Most customer interactions in a contact center don't exactly involve a suit and tie. Even the most informal conversation, however, must always maintain a professional tone.

When speaking with or emailing customers, agents want to come across as professional and as if they were having a face-to-face encounter. It enhances both their reputation and that of the business.

However, many conversations — such as a status check, follow-up response, or resolution confirmation — are by their very nature informal.

Agents should keep in mind the following advice to prevent them from veering into the unprofessional:

Don't say "no problem." If someone thanks you, you might feel that what you did wasn't a big deal, but keep that to yourself. It starts with "no" and is too casual. More importantly, it is too casual. Simply say, "You're welcome," in its place.
Be precise. The majority of people ask, "How are you?" without really wanting to know. By saying, "Hello, Louise," you can add a friendly, professional touch. How are things going at work?

Finish with a memorable statement. Have a good day" has lost all significance. Try a different approach: "Thank you for purchasing this item from us. I predict you'll enjoy it.

Having a discussion

Consider the most recent interaction you had with a stranger. Did you experience any awkward moments? Was the other person interesting to you? Was the other person interested in you? Were you happy that you spoke with the person?

Researchers in the field of social psychology have found that all of those questions have a positive conclusion.

Participants in a workshop the researchers ran to teach people in the neighborhood how to talk to strangers more effectively were surveyed both before and after the workshop.

According to the findings, people believed they would find their conversation partners interesting both before and after the conversation, according to study author Gillian Sandstrom, PhD, a senior lecturer in the psychology department at the University of Essex. However, she tells NBC News BETTER, they don't believe their partner will find them as fascinating in return. And almost everyone reports that the conversations went much better than they anticipated.

The findings were presented at the Society for Personality and Social Psychology Annual Convention in February after being published in the journal "Psychological Science" in the fall.

According to Sandstrom, the sample was a somewhat unusual group in that the attendees chose to participate in the event, making them motivated from the start to improve their conversational skills.

However, she asserts that the data would indicate that, even if conversations seem awkward, they are probably going better than you realize. Additionally, perhaps we can improve our ability to interact with strangers, whether they be a brand-new coworker, a friend of a friend, or the cashier at the grocery store.

Here's what Sandstrom and other experts want you to understand about how to communicate with strangers—and why doing so can be very beneficial to you.

It's challenging to converse with strangers because there are so many unknowns Speaking with a stranger is uncharted territory. It's harder and possibly more intimidating to talk to strangers than your partner, best friend, or mother, according to Sandstrom. We enter conversations believing that all these terrible things could occur.

Perhaps the other person talks too much. We may be speaking too much. They might stop operating. We could become bored. They could become bored. Uncomfortable silence might ensue. They could be attempting to flirt with me. They might be attempting to harm me in some way (which, according to Sandstrom, could be the reaction that is a holdover from our evolutionary past).

Context is important, According to Georgie Nightingall, conversation coach and founder of Trigger Conversations, an organization based in London that teaches people how to have more effective and meaningful conversations. In every situation, there are unwritten social norms that we usually try to abide by but aren't always sure about. Will revealing a certain fact about ourselves make us appear more credible or likable? Will being too bold impress or turn someone off?
“We want to be liked, or at least accepted by other people,” she says. “To not break these norms, we sometimes act like we’re treading on eggshells.”

We’re social beings. Even uncomfortable conversations are good for our wellbeing.

But, despite the awkward pauses, the missteps, and the unsure footing, talking to new people (even complete strangers we likely won’t see again) is good for us. Studies have shown that even small amounts of social interaction, like chatting with a stranger on the train, can improve mood.

In one study, researchers chose participants at random as they walked into a busy coffee shop in downtown Vancouver, telling some to try to strike up a conversation with the barista and others to fetch coffee as quickly as possible. Compared to the efficient group, the former group claimed to have left the coffee shop in a better mood and with a stronger sense of community. (The research was published in the "Social Psychological and Personality Science" journal in 2013).

According to study co-author Elizabeth Dunn, PhD, professor of psychology at University of British Columbia, it is impossible to determine from the data how this strategy for elevating mood compares to other approaches or how long the effect would last (Sandstrom was the other co-author). It's a low-hanging fruit, though. The conversations, continues Dunn, "add value."

To express their true selves, people want to connect with you on a real level.

Conversation expert George Nightingall, founder of TRIGGER CONVERSATIONS

A group of students were asked to carry counters around and keep track of all of their social interactions throughout the course of a day in a different study by Dunn and Sandstrom. The students reported higher levels of happiness and wellbeing as a result of having more social interactions.

According to Sandstrom, Nightingall, Dunn, and others, personality differences have a smaller impact on these claims than you might anticipate. Extroverts and introverts are both social beings, according to Nightingall.

According to Sandstrom, compared to extroverts, those who are more introverted frequently worry more in advance about how conversations will turn out. However, those discrepancies disappear when people discuss the advantages of conversation (according to what she and colleagues found in the aforementioned "Psychological Science" paper published last year). That research also looked at other personality differences besides introversion. “Things like self-esteem and rejection sensitivity didn’t matter,” Sandstrom says.

How to actually speak more confidently to strangers

Here are some tips, whether you're talking to a stranger on the elevator (yep, we went there), approaching someone at a networking event, or interacting with a friend of a friend you've never met before:

1. Be brave and less anxious

Sandstrom advises being brave and just doing it, even if it hurts. Both of you will likely enjoy it more than you anticipate and the other person will likely like you more than you anticipate.

Additionally, says Juliana Schroeder, PhD, an assistant professor at the Haas School of Business at the University of California, Berkeley, "don't be afraid to talk to someone who seems different from you." (She studies how people move through their social environments, including how interactions are influenced by language and mental capacity.) "Talking with someone who is different from you can be the most insightful and fascinating experience."

2. Show interest

Pose inquiries. Is the person sporting a standout piece of clothing? Why did they choose to attend the gathering you two are at? According to research, those who engage in conversation with others by asking more questions tend to be more well-liked. According to Sandstrom, a question can start or continue a conversation.

So start to wonder. Engage beginning with a brief and straightforward comment or exchange. Make appropriate, sincere verbal and/or physical responses while paying attention. Accept that there is no expectation that you will be actively participating; let it be/come naturally, and if you're relaxed, it will. If you feel under pressure, admit it (again, in all seriousness) and find a way out.

3. Don't be afraid to deviate from the plan

A question that makes your conversation partner think is engaging, so avoid the standard questions (what do you do, where do you live, etc.). You could also say something like, "I really don't understand this painting," or "I can't believe how crowded the train is right now." According to Nightingall, statements are requests to share curiosities.

And whether you're asking a question, replying, or making a statement, be authentic, she adds. "People want to get the real you so they can express the real them."

4. Give someone a compliment

It turns the focus to the other person and should make them feel wonderful, Sandstrom explains. When it comes to our anxieties about having conversations with people we don't know, we tend to be in our heads a lot, overthinking what we're doing wrong or what we could do wrong, she explains. Focusing the attention on the other person in those moments can help us get past those awkward spots, she says

5. Talk about something you both have in common

At the very least, you're in the same spot and experiencing the same weather. But don't be afraid to dig deeper and find more interesting commonalities: maybe you're from the same place, maybe you have a mutual friend, maybe you have a shared hobby, or maybe you work in similar roles.

"We tend to exaggerate how different people are from one another and how different they are from us, " Sandstrom adds. You actually probably share a lot of things in common, you just don't realize it yet.

6. Engage in more conversations with strangers. According to Sandstrom, the more you have, the more likely it is that you'll have fruitful

conversations. You become more adept at posing better queries and providing more insightful answers. She claims that although there is some skill involved, confidence is also gained by simply doing something more frequently. According to Schroeder, we worry about social rejection because we think the other person won't accept us or will ignore us. Contrary to popular belief, research indicates that most people are eager to start a conversation when asked to do so by another person. (Schroeder claims that we fail to account for social norms of politeness in our assumptions about fear.)

7. Avoid letting awkward situations get you down.

According to Sandstrom, the following are the steps in starting a conversation with a stranger: First, they give you a knowing look as if to say,

"Do I know you?" There's also the realization that they don't know you. "Wait, are you a weirdo?" comes next. When they get past all of that, they see that you are merely being cordial.

You must accept the possibility of temporary awkwardness, advises Sandstrom. However, if you continue, hopefully you'll reach the point where you're having a genuine conversation.

Selecting your clients

Finding the right customers who align with your creativity, goals, and values is the main goal of choosing customers.

Keep in mind that not every customer is a good customer.

The audience, according to Oscar Wilde, "was a total failure." The play was a great success. The audience and the play were clearly not a good fit!

What should you do, then, if your act, product, or service doesn't go over well? Change the audience or the offering? This question brings up a common issue that creative people have with marketing: the worry that a marketing strategy will result in a business that is driven by the market, a "lowest common denominator" approach to increase sales, and a "dumbing down" of the good or service. To put it another way, it will result in us "selling out" on our creative principles.

The biggest risk, in my opinion, is posed by the creative entrepreneur's wholesale rejection of marketing, market research, and market segmentation, which results in the loss of very beneficial resources. It stands to reason that in order to succeed on our terms, we must modify these methods to suit our needs.

In order to choose the most suitable audience, clients, or customers to meet our objectives, we must first be clear about our purpose. Any successful marketing strategy starts with choosing the right clients, or the people and businesses that match our goals, creativity, values, and economics. Any successful creative business starts with creating a special business formula that matches our best creativity with the right clients.

Not every client is a good client! Some clients are unrewarding in terms of trouble they cause. Some people won't like what we do, won't pay enough, or won't share our values. We must ignore these people and find better customers around which to build our creative enterprise. In short, marketing is about actively selecting and targeting the right kind of customers.

Trying to sell to anyone and everyone is not good marketing. Worse, it smacks of laziness and/or desperation, when what is needed is intelligent and creative thinking. It is when creative people in business choose the wrong kind of customers that they are faced with the choice of "selling cheap or selling out". Trying to build a feasible business around the wrong type of customers is doomed to failure.

Much of what we see and hear about marketing is about 'mass marketing' – the glitzy adverts for big companies that need to sell to the mass market. But the vast majority of creative enterprises don't need or want a mass market and so need to play a different game.

Market segmentation involves differentiating between different groups and types of customers so that we can select the right ones to approach and to deal with. By implication, it also means we can identify those segments of the market not to deal with.

So instead of thinking of the market as one mass, it's much more useful to think of it as a "mass of niches". Which market niches best suit our goods or services, our values, and our financial requirements is the crucial marketing question, then.

Business Link, the business support division of your local authority, and specialized creative industries support organizations for your own sub-sector or locality should all be able to assist you with business strategies that involve market segmentation.

When choosing customers, however, don't just consider locals. Sometimes the best clients are not right nearby. In fact, the more specialized your goods or services are, the harder it will likely be to attract enough of the right kinds of clients. One way to describe this approach is "narrow niche plus global reach."

Intentionally aiming for the Viridian Artists Gallery in New York, UK artist Sharon Mutch was successful thanks to the Passport to Export program from UK Trade and Investment (UKTI).

Instead of being thought of as consumers in and of themselves, galleries, bookstores, theaters, and other venues may be best understood as channels to consumers. To avoid the "sell cheap or sell out" trap, they too should be carefully chosen in the same manner and for the same reasons.

Target markets, demographics, psychographics, and other methods of defining who and what constitutes an ideal customer have been discussed extensively in marketing circles.

The idea mostly suggests that you choose the characteristics of a market that your company seems best suited to attract.
This straightforward strategy has always bothered me because it seems to focus on the lowest common denominator: who can we attract?

What if you shifted this perspective to ask, "Who do we deserve to work with?"

Have you ever given this question any thought? – What characteristics would our ideal clients possess?

I've been promoting this concept of an ideal customer for the past few years. The idea suggests behavior to me just as much as it does demographics.

And here's the other thing: Don't you deserve to work with clients who recognize the value of your special contribution?

Choosing your customers may seem a little egotistical to some, but that isn't the case at all. You had better step up your game if you want to collaborate with the industry's top players. Actually, it's a very humbling and centered concept.

The other day, I was discussing this very concept with a close friend. Morningstar Communications, owned by Eric Morgenstern, has had great success, and his client list reads like a "most wanted" list.

During a presentation to a group of business owners, Eric overheard me discussing my ideas on the ideal customer. He later explained to me how behavior has a significant impact on both the clients that a company seeks out and, perhaps more importantly, those that they do not.

"Our clients are kind, clever, and prosperous. A sustainable rate is two out of three.

"We've noticed:

Effective communication and our high caliber of service are valued by businesses that are "involved in the community."
Businesses that value "lifelong learning" frequently value good communication and our superior level of service.
Companies that are true leaders believe, ". . . an educated customer is a great customer."
Those are correlations that help us assess each individual prospect.

So much is a gut feeling . . . about the organization and its leadership, based on expertise and experience."

So, gather the troops and start asking about ideal customer behavior, traits and qualities that define success.

Begin by exploring personas that you don't want to work with. Persona is a term that takes its meaning from the idea of a theatrical role. In marketing the term is used to describe the common characteristics of a customer group much like the make up of a character in a play.

A client of mine did this exercise for his design and consulting business and was able to complete sketches of the kinds of clients they did not want to work with in such a way that it made it much easier to define what ideal looked like.

He framed characteristics that made up red flag customers using personas with names like Lottery Winners and Destined to Be Small. He even went so far as to list the clients with whom he would no longer be doing business.

The ironic thing is that until you have some clarity on this concept, it's far too simple to accept work and customers that take you away from the work you should be doing.

Saying something doesn't make it true, but success will elude you until you make an effort to identify, appreciate, and nurture who you truly are.

Instead of simply reacting to whoever shows up or attempting to sell to the most convenient people, choosing customers essentially involves being both active and discerning in relation to markets. Inspired by David Ogilvy's book "Confessions of an Advertising Man," the advertising agency Peppered Sprout adopted a proactive marketing stance. Instead of responding to local inquiries, as many businesses in their position do, they boldly chose their ideal client, Puma UK, and then came up with a plan to win them over.

Any creative business' marketing strategy must include selecting the right customers. Saying no to the wrong kinds of customers is the other side of the same coin and is equally important.

www.ingramcontent.com/pod-product-compliance
Lightning Source LLC
LaVergne TN
LVHW090136160826
845673LV00017B/2490

* 9 7 9 8 8 4 8 8 2 9 3 4 1 *